CIRCLE WISDOM

CIRCLE WISDOM

**Donna Mazzitelli • Melissa McQueen
• Janet Diederichs •**

MERRY DISSONANCE PRESS | CASTLE ROCK, CO

Circle Wisdom
Published by Merry Dissonance Press
Castle Rock, CO

Copyright © 2025 Donna Mazzitelli, Melissa McQueen, Janet Diederichs.
All rights reserved.

www.SeedsOfLightForAll.com

No part of this publication may be reproduced or transmitted in any form or by any means, electronic, mechanical, including photocopying, or by any information storage and retrieval system without written permission from Merry Dissonance Press, Donna Mazzitelli, Melissa McQueen, or Janet Diederichs, except for the inclusion of brief quotations in a review.

All images, logos, quotes, and trademarks included in this book are subject to use according to trademark and copyright laws of the United States of America.

FIRST EDITION
2025

Publisher's Cataloging-in-Publication
(Provided by Cassidy Cataloguing Services, Inc.)

Names: Mazzitelli, Donna, author. | McQueen, Melissa, author. | Diederichs, Janet, author.
Title: Circle wisdom / Donna Mazzitelli, Melissa McQueen, Janet Diederichs.
Description: First edition. | Castle Rock, CO : Merry Dissonance Press, [2025] | Series: Seeds of light collection.
Identifiers: ISBN: 9781939919779
Subjects: LCSH: Self-actualization (Psychology) | Circle--Psychological aspects. | Spirituality. | Mindfulness (Psychology) | Awareness. | Sacred space. | Self-realization. | Mind and body. | Mental health. | Change (Psychology) | Control (Psychology) | LCGFT: Self-help publications. | BISAC: BODY, MIND & SPIRIT / Inspiration & Personal Growth. | SELF-HELP / Spiritual.
Classification: LCC: BF637.S4 M39 2025 | DDC: 158.1--dc23

ISBN 978-1-939919-77-9

Book Interior and Cover Design © 2025
Art and Photography by Melissa McQueen, CreativeReflections.design
Cover and Book Design by Melissa McQueen, CreativeReflections.design
Editing by Donna Mazzitelli, WritingWithDonna.com
All Rights Reserved by Donna Mazzitelli, Melissa McQueen, Janet Diederichs, and Merry Dissonance Press

This book is dedicated to ALL working on behalf of the Divine Sacred Principle.

FOREWORD: A Note from Janet

I am excited to introduce you to what you already know but may not be aware of, the Circle. The Circle is a map, a tool for life. Its beingness is such a part of us that we don't see it. We override the awareness, thus missing the wisdom it holds.

Among the various Indigenous nations, Circle is a foundational blueprint, yet the approach to Circle may differ. As presented, what follows is based upon the lineage of my teachers.

I was made aware of Circle Wisdom, taught and passed on through the oral tradition. Grandmother Tú Moonwalker gave me the first foundational pieces. Others broadened and supported the information over the years. Thus, I must give credit in a most humble and respectful manner and with gratitude to: Grandmother Tú Moonwalker, Wisdom Carrier of Native American Apache and South American Lineages; Grandmother Láné Sáan Moonwalker, Wisdom Carrier of Yoeme and Apache Lineages; Grand Tia Blassa De Yah Lunata (Trudy Welty), Wisdom Holder and Teacher of the Ways of Mother Nature; and to the many participants in "The Philosophy of Universal Beingness Within The Whole." Honorable mention to Mary Jo Sumrall, my grounded mainstay and environmental guardian.

As I integrated Circle teaching, to the best of my intention I passed it on to friends and clients. In a session with Grandmother Tú, she held the imagery of a pebble dropped in a pond and its circular expansion through water. A gift to all for all. For more than a decade, two talented individuals continued to ask and wanted to learn and understand these teachings. During the Summer Solstice 2024, these two students approached me and asked if they could put this in writing. This held a deep responsibility for me to consider how they could impart this information in a manner that was not just words and facts, since it came to me through oral tradition and experience. I wanted to ensure that readers would have the same experience—felt through the entire body, clarified through the mind, and held in the heart as true. My belief is that what is being offered in the coming pages conveys this intention.

May I introduce to you Melissa McQueen and Donna Mazzitelli. They are the absolute reason for this book, as I am not a writer, poet, or artist.

> **Melissa**: photographer extraordinaire, graphic artist, environmental guardian
>
> **Donna**: author, editor, poet, one who carries hope in her nature

Their creative talents share the teachings and wisdom I've been honored to receive and work with in ways that engage the sensory system. Take a deep dive into the pictures, words, and poetry. Connect, relate, heal, and become whole.

With Gratitude to All Beings,

> **Janet Diederichs**
> Storyteller, Nature Guardian, and Teacher and Student of Universal Beingness Within The Whole

Gather round
The Circle awaits you.

You are invited to come as you are.
No matter what has happened in the past
Or is happening in the present
You are being called to enter.
This is your time—come.

Gather round
The Circle awaits you.

Here, you will find safety.
Here, you will find sanctuary.
Here, you will find solace.
For a time, you are encouraged to BE.
Within Circle's embrace, there is no judgment.
Unconditional Love and nurturance await you.
Acceptance is Circle's gift to you.

Gather round
The Circle awaits you.

Circle encourages you to see yourself
    in all your beautiful imperfection.
As a mirror reflects your image, Circle invites you to
    look deeply within.
Acknowledging your dark and your light
Your shadows and your knowing.

Gather round
The Circle awaits you.

Circle has much to teach you—
About life and living
About cycles and flow
About truth and illusion
About your connection to the ALL.

Gather round
The Circle awaits you.

We are all the same and each unique.
We are all equal and each a part of the whole.
We are all integral to the turning
From possibility to fulfillment
From revelation to transformation.

Gather round
The Circle awaits you.

Go with the flow
Feel the pull
Sense the potential
Join us now as we embark on
An exquisite journey of discovery.

Gather round and enter the Circle
This is your time.

BEGINNING OUR JOURNEY

The Circle has been a symbolic, geometric form since the beginning of time. From as far back as historically recorded, Circle has been used as a metaphor for the cycles of life and Earth's natural rhythms, a model for the most practical human tools, and a sacred symbol within every spiritual path.

In the coming pages, you are invited to expand your knowledge and experience the Circle in ways you may have never considered before. Your journey through this book has been designed to engage your senses. Let your body sway to the melodic rhythm of the poems, allow the colors and shapes of the images to wash over you, challenge your mind to contemplate concepts you may have not previously considered, and take the time to pause and breathe, asking that sacred space within you if it finds itself in a place of curiosity, peace, or remembrance.

Knowing that we all take in our world in different ways and that each of us benefits from being able to explore new or broadened concepts in more than one way, the following pages provide a variety of methods to engage with the information introduced. Each concept presented includes opportunities to take in a deeper understanding of the information shared, an invitation for personal participation through suggested activities, and moments for you to pause and reflect. This book is not meant to be devoured in one sitting or read only one time. You are encouraged to return to these pages over and over. Through such an approach, it is our intention that you will be surprised, delighted, and invigorated each time you return, deepening your understanding of both Circle and yourself.

It is time for us to begin. We invite you to gather a journal or notebook, perhaps a warm cup of tea, and get comfortable as you turn to the next page and join us on this most profound journey.

CHAPTER 1
CIRCLE IS EVERYWHERE

*Circle is everywhere
See it out there*

Circle is in nature—
In the sun
In the moon
In a flower's pattern
In a ripple of water

Circle is everywhere
  See it in here

Circle is in you—
In your eyes
In your belly button
In the cells of your body
In your body's openings where you receive and release

Circle is everywhere
See it all around

Circle is with you each day—
In your glass, your cup, your plate, your bowl
In your tires and wheels
In the clock on your wall
In the rings on your fingers

*Circle supports you
Circle is a part of you
Circle is everywhere*

Observe the Circle

As reflected in "Circle Is Everywhere," we can find expressions of Circle throughout our world, within ourselves, and in our everyday lives. Take some time now to experience Circle for yourself.

Start by slowing down and focusing your attention on how deeply Circle is already integrated within your life. Become aware of your surroundings. Spend at least five minutes walking around your living space, discovering all the places you find Circle. Take yourself outdoors and spend time observing the many expressions of Circle you encounter.

Once you've spent time indoors and outside, take a moment to consider how you might record what you've discovered, doing so in a manner that feels most freeing or creative to you. Examples of how to record your discoveries:

- Make a simple list in your journal or notebook
- Take photos of what stood out to you both indoors and outdoors
- Create a collage
- Draw pictures

There is no need to hurry through this activity. Take as much time as you need to appreciate and find your personal way to capture what you've encountered. Have fun and let yourself enjoy this experience.

CIRCLE - THE FOUNDATION OF LIFE

Having now spent time discovering Circle around you, you may ask, "Why is Circle so prevalent?" At its core, Circle is the foundation of life itself. Even before humans inhabited the planet, Circle was a part of creation. The circular rotation of planet Earth creates day and night as well as the cycle of seasons. The elements work together in a circular pattern, creating our weather through the process of water, evaporation, cumulation, and rain. Circle is seen in the smallest of visible objects—all the way down to the circular orbit of electrons around the nucleus of cells. It is seen in the largest of visible objects, such as the sun and moon.

Since the earliest days of human existence, Circle has been an inherent part of our lives. A fire was often built in the center of a circular clearing to ensure it wouldn't spread, with people gathered around the fire, allowing each to be equally warmed by it. Even the light created by the fire spread evenly in a circle, enabling those gathered to be seen and to see each other.

Without needing to put words to our experience, our human bodies have always felt connected to and loved being with Circle. Even ancient stones were usually laid in a circular formation for community gathering spaces. Such configurations offered a sense of nurturance and support.

Circle became a beneficial tool, ingrained in the everyday life of humanity, whether for the fire used to warm their bodies and cook their food or by rolling logs to move supplies that were too heavy to carry. Eventually, with the invention of the wheel, people themselves were able to move from place to place.

For centuries, the significance of Circle has been demonstrated through our language, yet we may not have ever considered that significance. Who hasn't heard of the legendary Knights of the Round Table? In King Arthur's court, the round table was essential for his knights to be seen and to feel equal to one another. Today, businesses and organizations often hold meetings that are referred to as roundtable discussions. Whether seated at a round table or not, it's implied that the discussion will be one where all attendees are encouraged to participate. A round table promotes equity and balance—everyone sitting around the table can be seen and heard.

In any group setting, we each come with our own experiences, biases, and preferences, which filters our view of every circumstance. Sitting in a circle allows us to consider other viewpoints and encourages us to work from a place of fair and equitable exchange, bringing the differing perspectives together to come to mutually beneficial resolutions. By communicating and processing through Circle, we are able to move beyond our own individuality and instead work collectively.

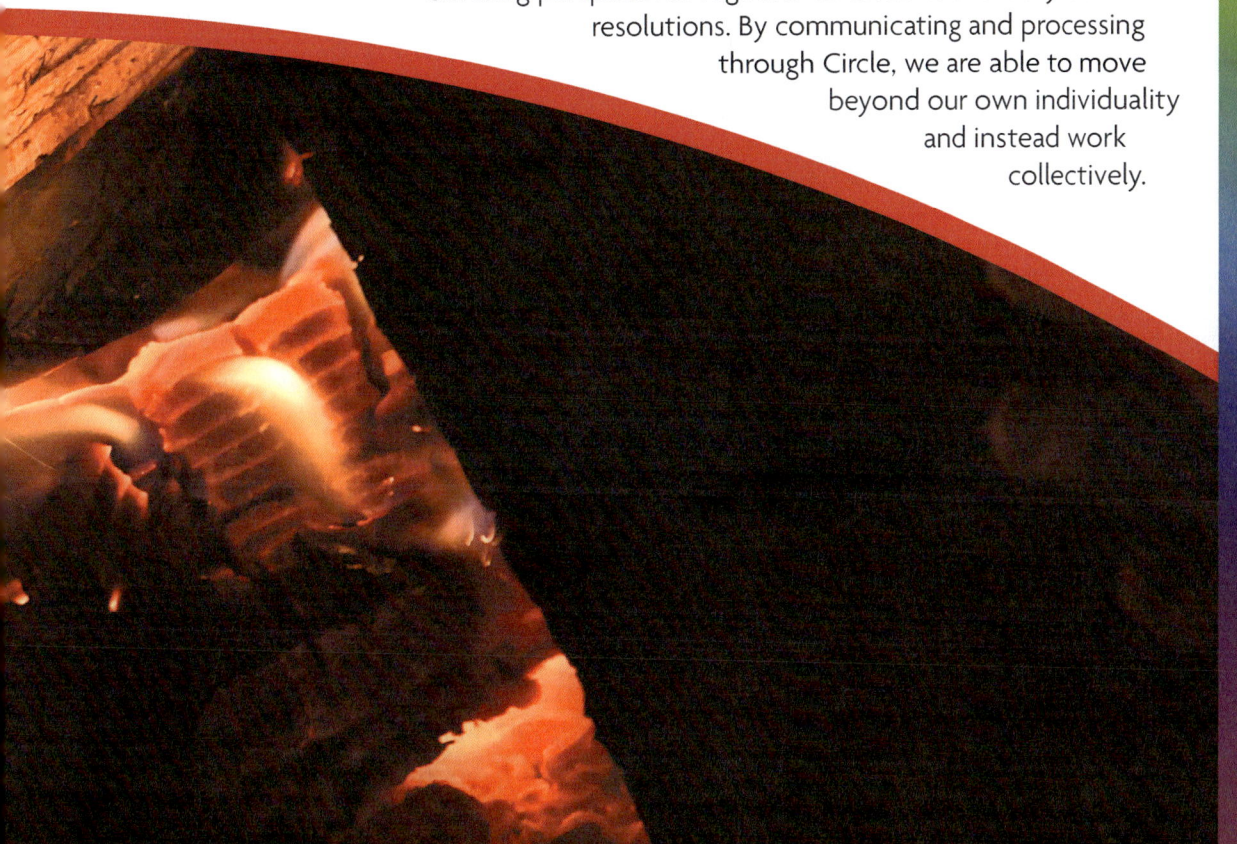

GUIDED MEDITATION

Begin the journey with Circle. I am here—here I am.

Find a quiet place away from your daily responsibilities to be with the meditation's guidance. Gather a cushion, blanket, and anything else that will make it comfortable for you to be in a seated position. Allow time for the meditation and the reflection that follows. Be sure to have your journal and pen available to record your experience.

LISTEN

Scan the QR Code for the Guided Meditation.

REFLECTION
Journaling - Connection

As shared in this opening chapter, Circle is ever present and everywhere. Circle has and always will support you.

Using the questions below as a guide, take some time to write about your experience during the meditation and with this chapter.

1. Describe the environment you visualized during the meditation. What makes this environment a place of acceptance and connection for you?

2. In drawing the Circle, what sensations did you experience?

3. Which senses were you able to connect with at Circle's Center? Describe your experience.

4. Who joined you in the Circle? Did any surprise you? How did you feel in their presence?

5. How has what you've read and experienced in this chapter changed the ways you view Circle?

CHAPTER 2
ENTERING THE CIRCLE

Center Yourself

Circle invites you
To step into it

In this first conscious encounter
Walk to the center
Stand in the middle and turn
Clockwise—turn round and round
Move with its flow

Circle asks you to stay for a time
Sit and center yourself at its center
Stretch out your arms
And feel its sacred space
Circle holds you in its embrace

At its center, experience Circle's heartbeat
Moving around you
Within you
And with you
Expand your heart
And join with the rhythm
Of Unconditional Love

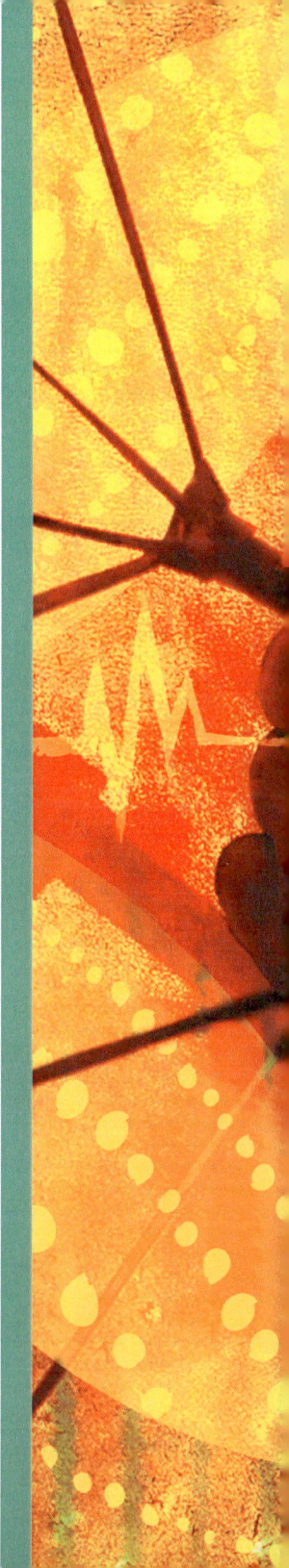

This is the time for awareness
To sense your surroundings
To feel yourself in relation to Circle's beingness
Above, below, in front, behind, side to side, within
Circle welcomes you and joins with you
As Circle knows you, so too will you come to know Circle
Circle has drawn you in—
allow yourself to merge with Circle

Feel the Circle from Its Center

Take a moment to view the world around you from Circle's Center. Allow your heart to open and to receive. Circle has many gifts to offer.

Start by setting up a circle on the floor or ground. This can be achieved in multiple ways: an adult size hula-hoop, yarn, or rope set in a circle, using a circular rug or creating a circle around you with stones, shells, or any items from nature. As described in the poem, step into your Circle, bringing your journal with you, and move to the center. While still standing, slowly turn clockwise, focusing on all you can see directly in front of you as you move.

Take a seated position at the center of the Circle. Before doing anything further, take a few moments to journal the details of your observations and any feelings that came up.

Stretch out your arms and feel the containment of the Circle around you. Now, close your eyes and place your hands on your heart. Take time to feel your own heartbeat. Breathe in and out slowly and feel your breath. As you sit in this rhythm, expand your awareness beyond your own body and feel the heart of the Circle. Are you able to sense the two rhythms begin to merge? Open your eyes and journal about your experience.

How do you feel? Does your body feel comfortable in this space? Do you feel Circle's presence and its welcoming embrace?

AT CIRCLE'S CENTER

Circle creates connection with others and with ourselves. Although our conscious mind believes complexity is better, bigger is better, more is better, Circle invites us to feel the simplicity of its beingness in our bodies.

As humans, we need connection—genuine connection that we can feel rather than artificially created constructs of connection we participate in, such as social media and technology. Our need for genuine connection is the main reason we are drawn to sit in a group Circle or around an outdoor fire. We may not realize what is happening, but we feel that connection to each person—it's an unconscious bodily response to the nurturance Circle's blueprint provides.

WE ARE LOVED. WE ARE ONE.

Circle anchors us to the Earth and connects us to everything—to the ALL of life. When we sit alone at Circle's Center, we have a visceral response to it in our bodies. We may feel safe, comfortable, and embraced. Or we may feel extremely uncomfortable.

Circle's Center is a place that encourages us to transform and evolve.

Because Circle holds Unconditional Love, Circle meets us where we are, without judgment or conditions. If, at Circle's Center, we feel pushed, unsettled, or uncertain, and whether we accept Circle's invitation or not, Circle is ALWAYS there to support us.

Transformation

From the moment we are conceived
    to the event of our birth,
Our bodies begin the process
    that eventually leads to our death.
Programmed and unconscious,
    transformation is happening.
Day in and day out,
    without our awareness,
Our bodies' natural processes
    are in a constant state of change.

One of the most beautiful representations of
    this programmed process is a butterfly.

From egg to caterpillar to chrysalis
    to its final expression of BEing.
A transformational process—
    a metamorphosis—must occur.
Within the chrysalis,
    the caterpillar breaks down,
Becoming a soup of unique potential that forms
    into the parts of the butterfly.
Once formed,
    the butterfly must break out to survive.
Through the discomfort of release,
    the butterfly's wings gain strength,
    enabling it to fly, to soar,
And to be the beautiful BEing
    it was programmed to become.

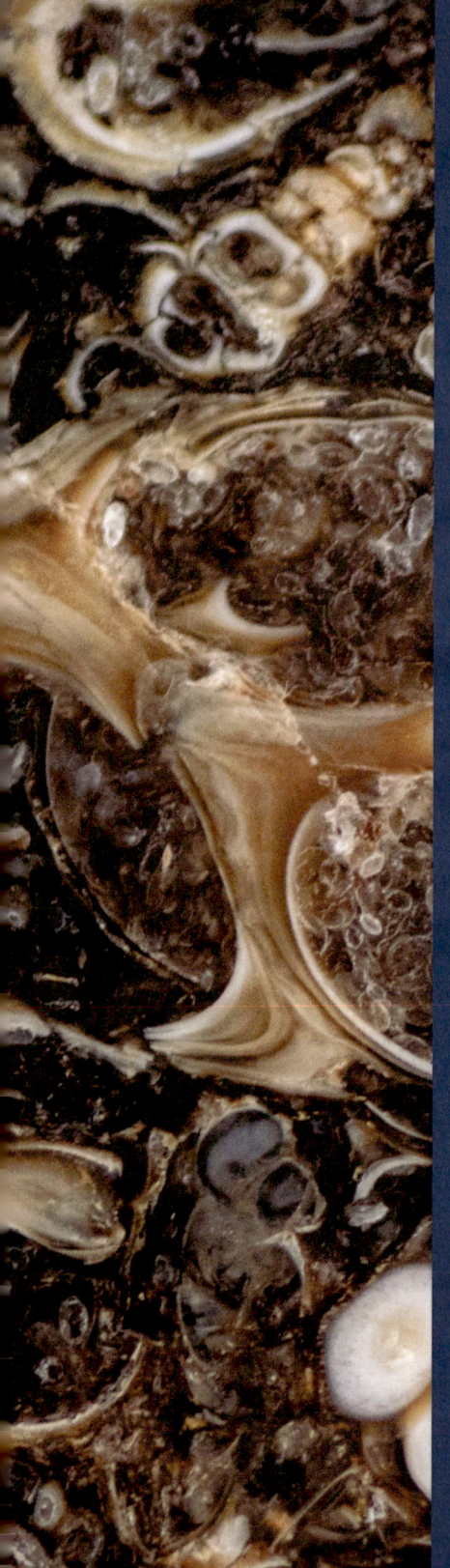

Like the butterfly
    that is programmed to be what it is,
We are programmed to age—
    an unconscious and inevitable
    transformation in our lifetime.

Yet, as humans,
    we have been given the additional gift
Of conscious transformation.
Mentally, emotionally, and spiritually,
    we are offered
        the opportunity to change and grow.

At Circle's Center,
    we are especially encouraged
        to become.

Transformation isn't always easy.
In transformation,
    something dies and is reborn.
The energy of destruction transforms
    into the creation of another.
To release what no longer serves us,
    bringing us the blessings of our unique potential.
What is required is our willingness—
    To be open to the possibilities
        and take the steps necessary
    To become the fullest expression
        of our BEingness.

Evolution

Transformation over time—
    Subtle or dramatic
    Circular or spiral
    Personal or universal
    In one's lifetime or over generations
    Through eons of time
    Creating shifts.
This is evolution.

Stop and look back—
    Consider what is different now
    As compared to what was before.
    See life from a new perspective.
This is evolution.

Pause to acknowledge—
    What has been lost
    What has been gained
    What has been learned
    What has been forgotten
    What has become.
This is evolution.

Evolution is growth.
Evolution is change.
Evolution is inevitable.

A series of transformations
    Resulting in something new
        Something forever altered
Transformation and evolution—
    Intertwined for eternity.

Unconditional Love

Circle's Center holds Unconditional Love.
    You are an expression of that love.
You came into the world with this knowing.
    You came into the world as pure Light and Love.

As we grow, we lose the awareness—
    That we are not separate from Unconditional Love,
    And that everything and everyone is connected.
This loss is part of our shared human experience.
    But we can re-remember.

Allow Circle, an energetic container of this love,
    To hold you and help you remember.
Allow Unconditional Love to flow through you—
    Feel its gentle waves coming from all directions.
    Without judgment,
    Without the need to do or change anything.
Allow yourself to experience Circle's Unconditional Love.

At Circle's Center, you are encouraged to BE.
    You are offered the gift to receive this expansive love
Through your heart and lungs—
    Breathe in this immense Unconditional Love.
    Breathe out this unlimited Unconditional Love.

Give yourself permission to know
    You are Unconditional Love.
        You ARE
            And always
                Have been.

GUIDED MEDITATION

Experience Circle more deeply at Circle's Center.

Find a quiet place away from your daily responsibilities to be with the meditation's guidance. If you've created a Circle space, use that space for the meditation. To begin, take a seated position within your Circle space. Allow time for the meditation and the reflection that follows. Be sure to have your journal and pen available to record your experience.

LISTEN

Scan the QR Code for the Guided Meditation.

REFLECTION
Journaling - Connection

Circle's Center is a place that encourages us to transform and evolve. Circle meets us where we are, without judgment or conditions, offering us Unconditional Love.

Using the questions below as a guide, take some time to write about your experience during the meditation and with this chapter.

1. At Circle's Center, how did the observation of your heartbeat, your center, change as you listened? Describe the sensations and awarenesses you experienced.

2. As you sat in Circle's Center, what did you feel? Describe your experience through your senses.

3. When you consider that Circle holds you in the same manner you held something you deeply love, how did that feel? Did you feel resistance or were you drawn to this experience?

4. Circle holds the finite self and the Infinite Divine. Were you able to connect with or recognize both? Describe your experience.

5. After reading this chapter related to Circle's Center, what stood out to you?

CHAPTER 3
DIRECTIONS: Movement Around the Circle

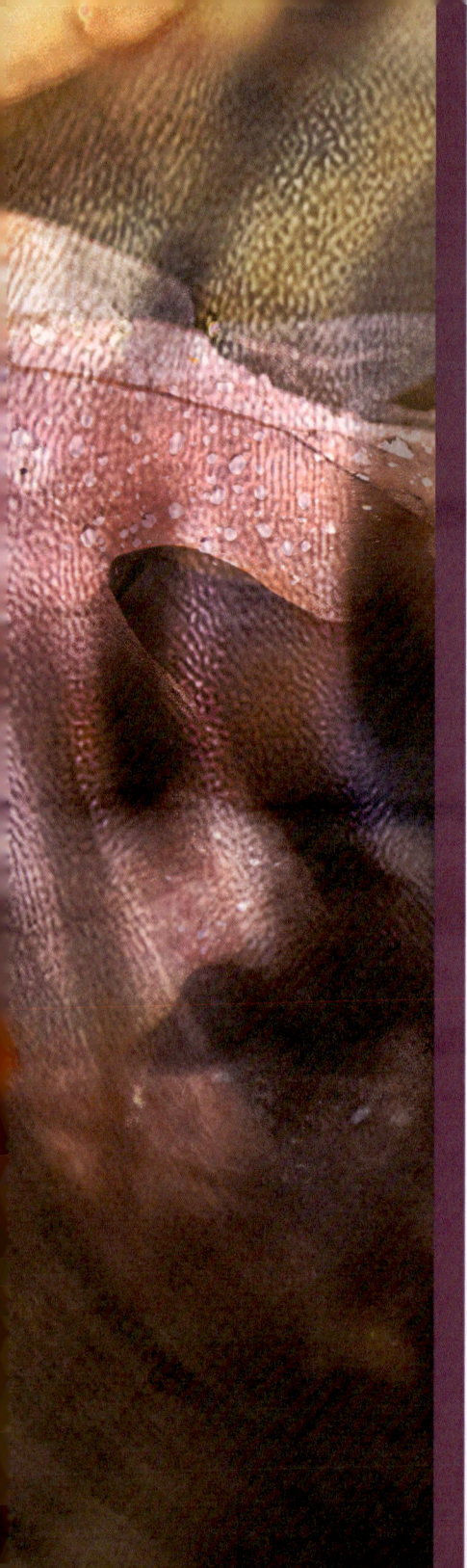

Move with Circle's Directions

Circle's call urges us
    to begin our journey
To learn about this ancient geometry
    and our relationship to it.

*In this first encounter,
    we meet the directions*

We enter from the **East**,
    which encourages us to BE.

*This is the place that calls us to see
    our right to exist
Along with our unique
    contribution to the Whole.*

*Like a puzzle piece
    needed to complete a picture,
You are a necessary and essential
    element to the ALL of life.*

*Your uniqueness makes you an
    indispensable piece within
      the Universal puzzle
        of BEingness.*

We move clockwise and meet the **Southeast**,
    a place of learning.
Within Circle, learning is seen as expansion
    to consider new perspectives
    to contemplate the possibility of change
    to shed light on
        what we previously could not see
        and what is vital to retain.
Learning encourages us to grow.

In the **South**, we acknowledge
    our ability to grow.
Although growth can feel chaotic,
    we are offered a rhythm and pattern
    through the cycle of days, seasons, years,
    and even our lifetime.
We are stretched in body, mind, and essence
    to BEcome.
And like the rings within a tree,
    we can look back at any point in time
    to see how far we've come.

Arriving in the **Southwest**,
    we face that as humans
    we will make mistakes.
Yet, this is the place that guides us to
    self-compassion
        rather than self-judgment
    and self-acceptance
        rather than self-rejection.
Mistakes teach us humility and patience
    with ourselves and others.
Reminding us that as humans
    there is no such state as perfection.

Sitting in the **West**,
    we look back to where we began
        in the East.
Like the sun rises and arches across the sky
    from one horizon to the other,
        we arrive in the place of pause.
Sunrise and sunset
    are the most celebrated times of day.
Here, we honor what we've experienced
    and accomplished thus far
And review, reflect on, and assess
    what will lead to further change.
This reflection and
    assessment leads to change.

Approaching the **Northwest**,
    we recognize
        we have much to be grateful for.

SEE *the beauty that surrounds you*
TOUCH *the textures within nature*
SMELL *the fresh morning air*
TASTE *the juicy goodness of fresh berries*
LISTEN *to your breath that gives you life*

Focus on the plentitude,
    using ALL of your senses.
Feel the abundance in your life,
    remembering your most primal senses
        of intuition and
        your recognition of energies.
In gratitude,
    appreciate the gifts of BEing alive.

The **North** reflects our wisdom
   from all who have come before us—
      our ancestors and lineage
   and ALL we have gained during
      our journey so far.
Our right to die is offered to us here
   when our human suit no longer serves us,
      to become part of the lineage and
         move into the next
            expression of ourselves.

In the **Northeast**, we are offered
   the opportunity to let go of
   what no longer serves us.
This is the place of reciprocity and negotiation
   of Fair and Equitable Exchange,
Where we ultimately reach
   Completion and Closure.

From here we step into
   the mystery and the unseen.

As we reapproach the **East**,
*we are given entry to
the* **Center**.

*This centermost point leads
to our evolution and transformation—
as we sit in Unconditional Love
and hear the words:*

"You are LOVED.

"You are ESSENTIAL."

Returning to the **East** to exit
    We know we are not the same
        as when we entered.
    Forever transformed,
        we begin again.

From this new place of beingness,
    we are invited to
        step into the East
            once more
And the cycle of our evolution
    begins again and continues.

DIRECTIONS: Movement Around the Circle

The directions in the Circle hold Universal Laws and Principles, which are the basic rights of every being. As is described in the opening piece to this chapter, each direction holds a specific right or set of rights. The following pages include an activity to connect with the rights inherent in each direction of the Circle. Taking a moment to sit with the Circle below will prepare you to move through Circle's flow.

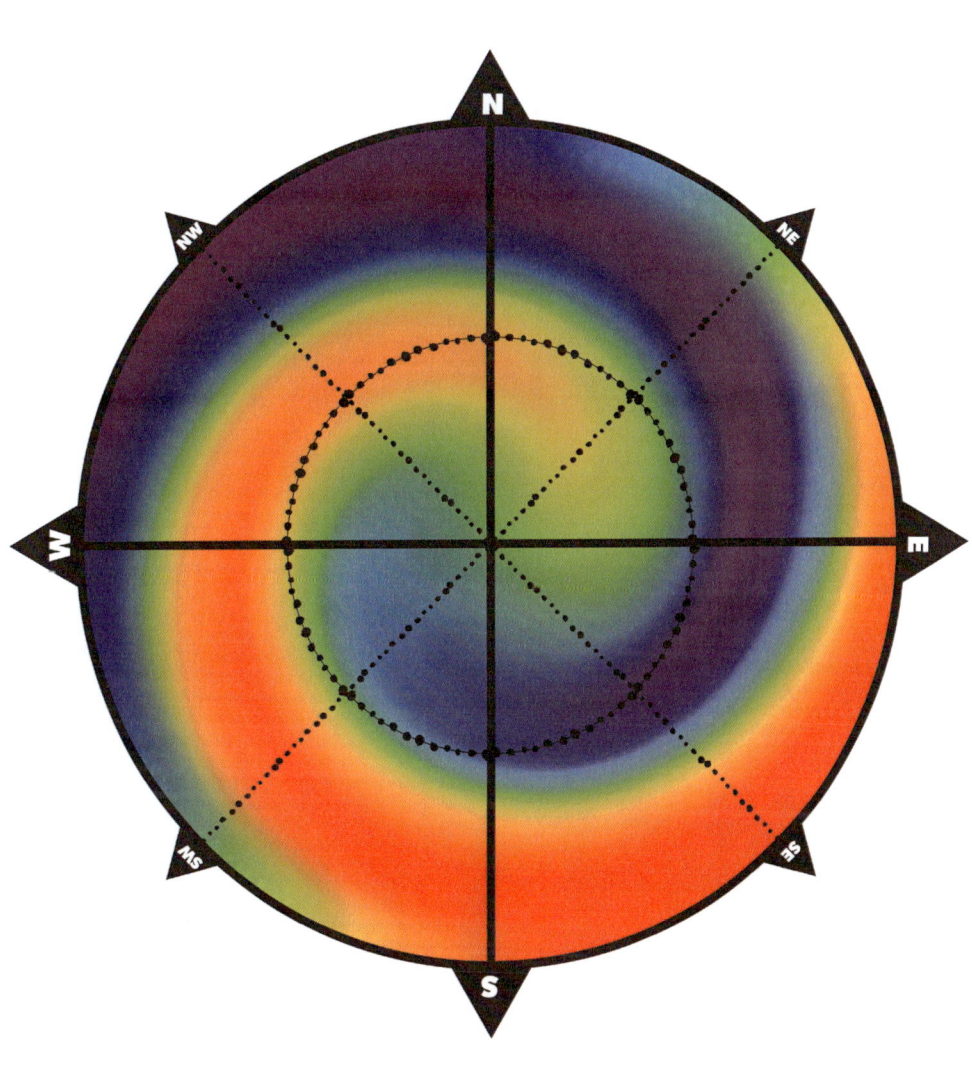

DIRECTIONS: Movement Around the Circle

Before beginning, pause to acknowledge Circle as a sacred space. Then place your finger on each direction as it is described. As you pause on the direction, consider the right it holds. What do you feel in your body? What images come to mind? Do you feel drawn to or feel resistance to that principle?

Beginning in the East is the **Right to Be**. Every being on the planet has the right to exist. The right to exist is the foundation to our experience of every other direction and the rights each hold.

Moving in a clockwise direction, you come to the **Southeast**, the **Right to Learn**. Ongoing throughout our lives, learning is inevitable. We gain new experiences each day, which allow us to consider how we see and understand the world.

Continuing clockwise, you arrive at the **South**, the **Right to Grow**. Like a tree growing deeper roots and shooting upward toward the sky, we have the right to expand our awareness and elevate our beingness.

As we approach the **Southwest**, we come to the **Right to Make Mistakes**. What a beautiful gift Circle offers us to see that a mistake is not failure. It is another step in the learning process that helps us move forward with acceptance and self-compassion.

On to the **West**, a space that allows the **Right to Assess and Change**. At the halfway point in the Circle, we take a pause and reflect upon where we started and what has occurred, to assess what we might do differently as we continue. This is a place to recognize what we have learned and choose to carry forward.

Stepping into the **Northwest**, we rest with the **Right to Blessings and Gratitude** and the **Right to Awareness**. This is a space to acknowledge our blessings and the abundance in our lives. Here, may we also find gratitude for our continuing life and become aware of the many gifts that surround us.

In the **North**, we encounter the **Right to Wisdom** and the **Right to Die**. Movement around the Circle continues infinitely. With each rotation, we learn and gain wisdom that prepares and sustains us for the next cycle around the Circle.

At the **Northeast**, we come to the **Right to Completion and Closure** as well as the **Right to Fair and Equitable Exchange**. This provides the opportunity to drop the weight of what holds us back or release with gratitude what is now complete. In addition, it holds the gift of reciprocity, giving and receiving mutually beneficial offerings.

Returning to the **East**, we take a step into **Circle's Center,** a space with the **Right to Unconditional Love** and the **Right to Transform and Evolve**. Along with the attributes shared in Chapter 2, Circle's Center provides a safe space for us to gain a 360-degree perspective of each revolution we have traveled.

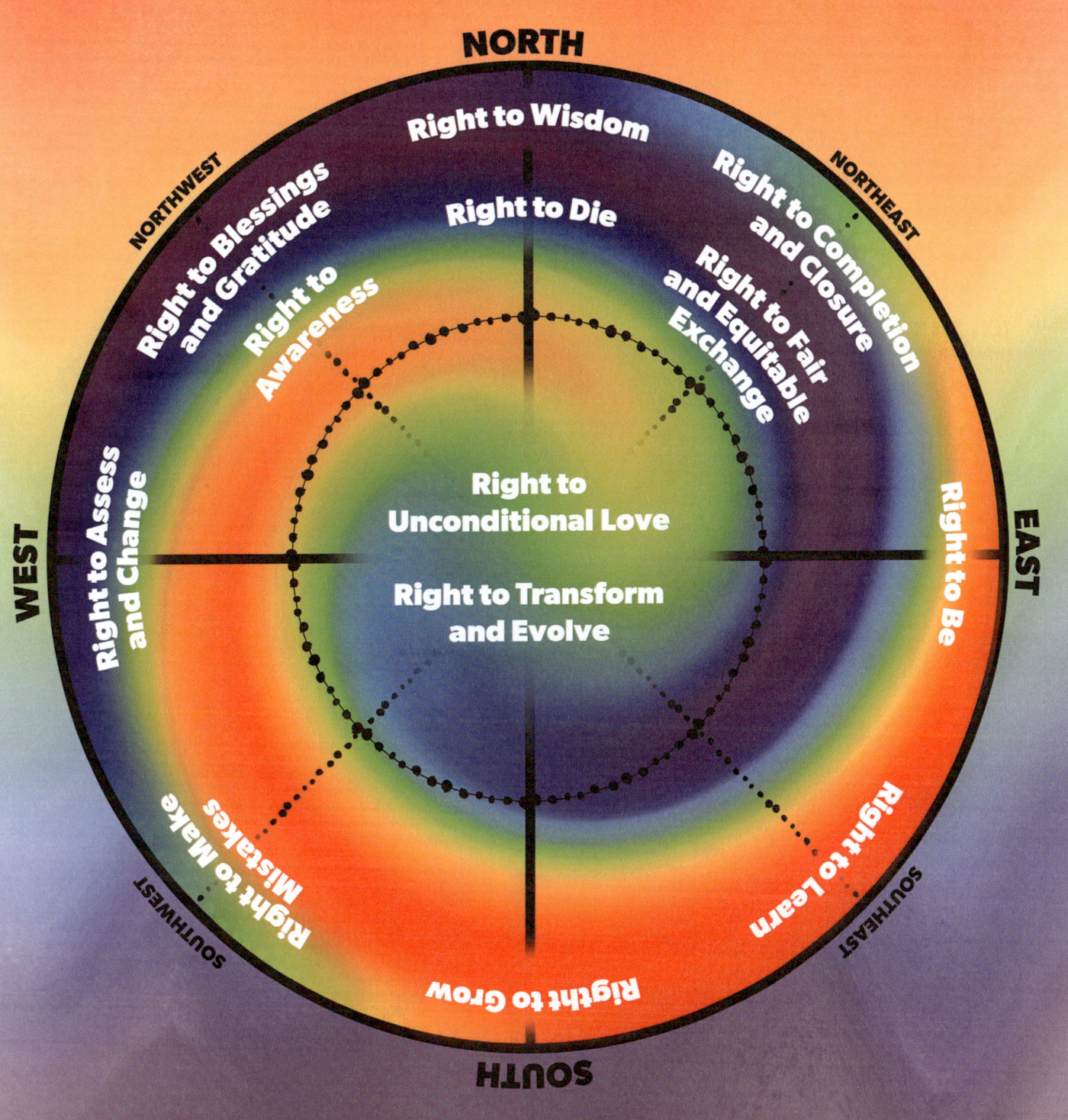

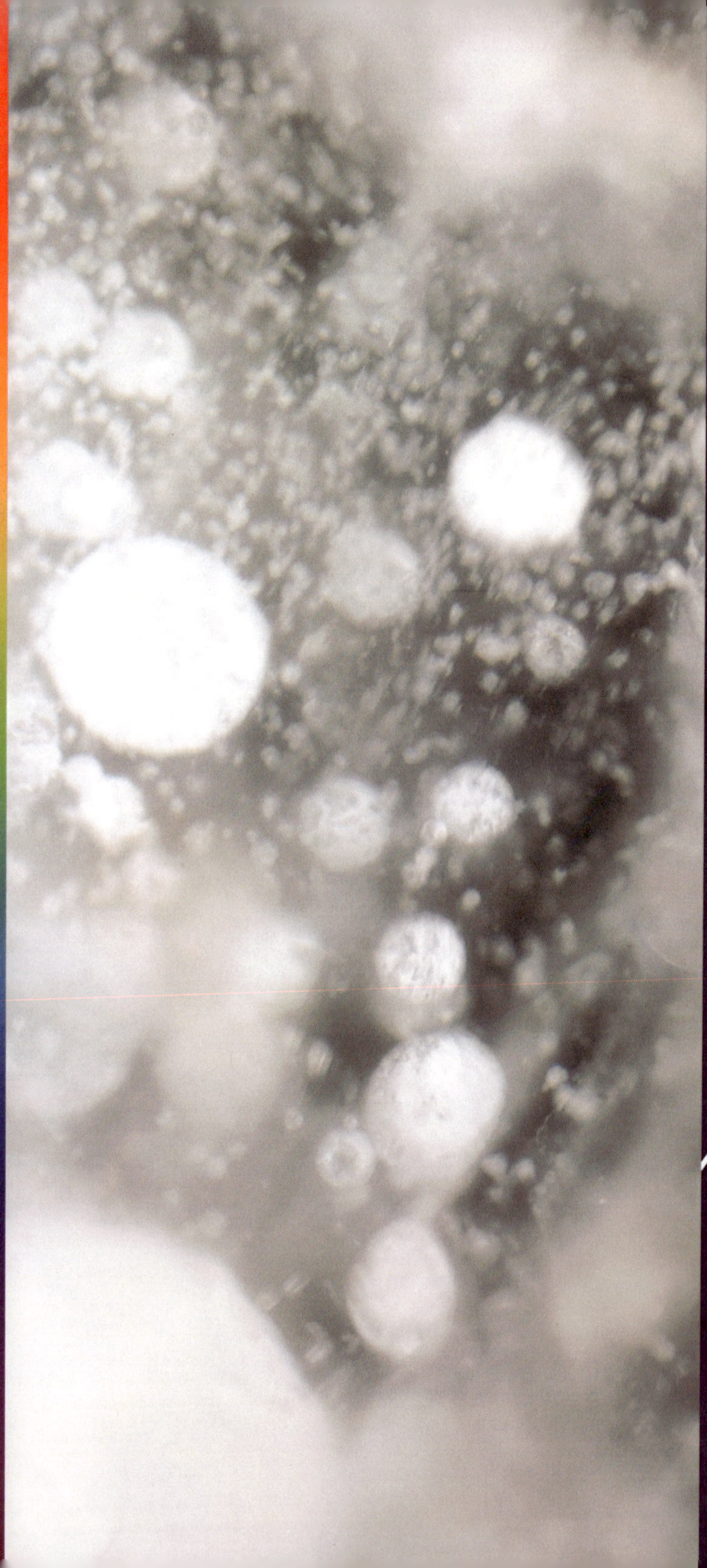

GUIDED MEDITATION

An opportunity to experience Circle's directions.

Find a quiet place away from your daily responsibilities to be with the meditation's guidance. If you've created a Circle space, use that space for the meditation. To begin, take a seated position within your Circle space. Allow time for the meditation and the reflection that follows. Be sure to have your journal and pen available to record your experience.

LISTEN

Scan the QR Code for the Guided Meditation.

REFLECTION
Journaling - Connection

Beginning in the East and moving in a clockwise direction, each of Circle's directions is a pathway to understanding more about ourselves and life. The directions provide guideposts along the way, offering gifts inherent in each direction.

1. As you entered the East, the place of new light, of new beginnings, what sensations did you feel in your body? What thoughts and emotions emerged?

2. As you traveled to the South, the place of growth and expansion, what sensations did you feel in your body? What thoughts and emotions arose?

3. As you moved to the West, the place of reflection and looking back, what sensations did you feel in your body? What thoughts and emotions did you experience?

4. As you continued to the North, the place of completion and wisdom, what sensations did you feel in your body? What thoughts and emotions did you encounter?

5. As you returned to the East and continued to the Center, where we can see all the directions, what sensations, thoughts, and emotions did you feel?

CHAPTER 4
CREATING A SACRED SPACE

Safe Within

Circle offers us a sacred space
    To be with ourselves
    To feel seen, cherished, and loved.
Circle's beingness holds a boundary
Which helps us consider the finite within
    And the infinite beyond

Within Circle, you are supported
Within Circle, you are shielded and protected
Within Circle, you are encouraged
    To consider your own beingness
To discover the SACRED YOU within You

Within Circle, you are safe
  To look within yourself
To observe, with compassion and curiosity
  The gems and gold within
Along with the cracks and fissures
  Created while living the human experience.

We are a mixture of light and dark,
  Of happiness and grief,
  Of joy and sorrow,
  Of empathy and judgment.
As humans, it's impossible not to experience
  The full range of being human.
Feel this spectrum without self-chastisement.
Hold yourself within Circle's sacred embrace
Take in Circle's Unconditional Love for you.

*Beyond Circle lies the infinite
Which includes ALL OTHER.*

*You are separate yet part of the whole
Which includes all BEings seen and unseen,
    Stationary and mobile,
      Past, present, and future.*

*Although part of everything
Circle reminds us to not overstep
To stay within our own boundary.*

*As we honor and respect ourselves,
And work within our personal sacred space
    To heal what is broken within,
    To nurture and nourish our gifts,
    To become the fullest expression of ourselves
Circle requires that we honor and respect ALL BEings
And allow ALL OTHER to do the same.*

*This is the way to discover and shine our Light
    To enlighten ourselves
        To enlighten ALL
            To create balance
                And join Universal Flow*

Your Sacred Space

Consider your surroundings, including a place within your home, an outdoor space, or a building, where you go to take time away from day-to-day life. A place of sanctuary that offers you a sense of safety and solitude. A place where you can be alone. A place where you can come and be present. Do you have such a place?

If so, within those surroundings, what elements make you feel that sense of security and sanctuary? And why? Take a moment to describe in your journal this space, the elements within, and how they make you feel.

Take note of your senses within this space—what do you see, hear, smell, and feel? Do you sit in the sunlight, play music, light a scented candle, wrap yourself in a blanket, or maybe submerse yourself in a warm bath?

If you don't have such a place, we invite you to create one for yourself. Consider where and what you would surround yourself with. Even if it can't be a permanent designated space, are there items you could gather and bring with you each time you want to create a personal sanctuary?

Time Within Your Sacred Space

Create some time to be in your sacred space. Although it may not look like a circle wherever you are, Circle's beingness is present. We invite you to create a physical representation of Circle within your space. It might be a rug, a hula-hoop, a long piece of ribbon or yarn that can be laid out in a circle. Once you have set your Circle, do you feel a deeper level of support? Can you feel the Unconditional Love and acceptance that Circle offers? Do you feel more grounded, rooted, and anchored? Are you comfortable in your body, is your mind relaxed? Do you feel connected to an energy beyond yourself? Do you feel other subtle changes or none at all? Describe your experience.

Stay as long as you need. When you are ready to leave, thank the Circle and your sacred space for the gifts you received.

CREATING A SACRED SPACE

As you allowed Circle to enwrap you once again, did you begin to feel the blanketed comfort its boundary provides? This protection is not a barrier or wall that stands between you and *all other*; it creates a filter similar to a reef protecting an ocean cove. Coral reefs filter out the water's toxins and provide a break from the destructive waves, creating a calm, clear oasis in the vastness of the ocean. Circle offers us a space that sifts out the constant waves of overwhelming, external static and noise to create a tranquil sanctuary where Light and Love easily flow through.

When you surround yourself with Circle, it provides a safe space to consider your own beingness. As you engage with Circle's beingness, it gently requests that all parts of you—mind, body, and essence—be present. Circle invites each part to come into alignment, bringing you to a place of peace within yourself, while reminding you that you are also one with the Divine.

You have now sat in Circle's Center, felt its embrace, walked along its boundary, and learned about each of the Universal Laws and Principles held in its directions. From the safety within Circle, you can focus your attention on the rights Circle allows you and others. Circle's boundary gently reminds us that we must honor and respect the sacred space encircling *all other*.

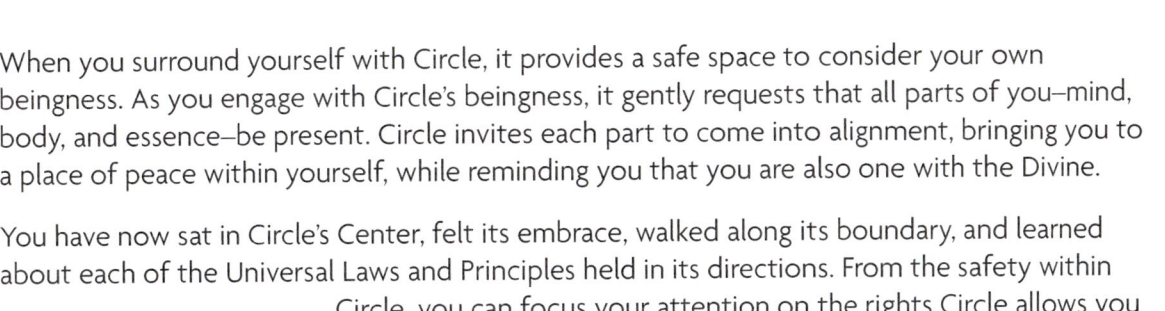

Open Invitation

The invitation is always open
    To return to Circle
        And feel it once more
    To walk its circumference
    To move to its Center
Surrounded with Love and Light
    Gently held within Circle

A sacred space—
    A place of safety
        That filters out the static of life
    A place of creativity
        Encouraging your imagination to play
    A place of peace
        Reminding you of your sacredness
    A place to return to
        Until you realize you can
            Forever remain

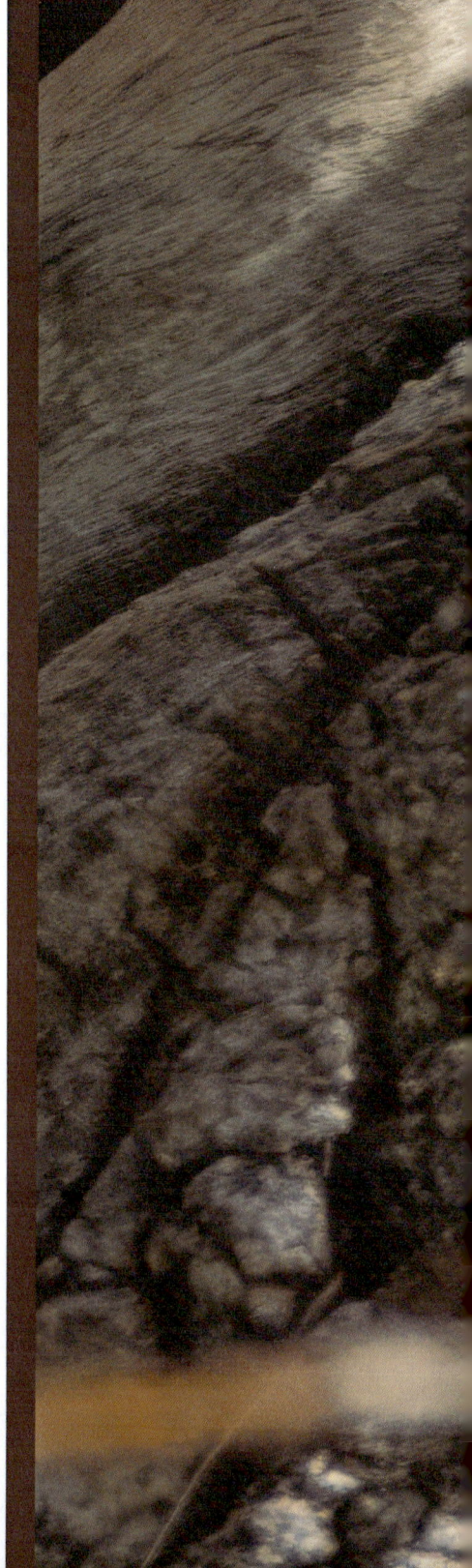

Here, you are allowed to go deep within yourself
*   To request every part of you*
*   Mind, body, spirit*
*   To come*
*   Be present*

Together, in alignment
*   They create the opportunity to reach*
*   Your highest potential*
*   And softly ask you*
*   To become a beacon*
*   That guides others*
*   To do the same*

GUIDED MEDITATION

Circle offers a place of sanctuary that is always here for us.

Find a quiet place away from your daily responsibilities to be with the meditation's guidance. Gather a cushion, blanket, and anything else that will make it comfortable for you to be in a seated position. Allow time for the meditation and the reflection that follows. Be sure to have your journal and pen available to record your experience.

LISTEN

Scan the QR Code for the Guided Meditation.

REFLECTION
Journaling - Connection

Circle creates a place of comfort and safety. Rather than solid, rigid boundaries it provides a protective filter where you can be with yourself away from life's static. A sanctuary where Light and Love flow.

1. When you visualized your garden of thoughts and feelings, what did you observe? What did you feel?

2. As you connected with your breath in Circle, what did Circle help you release? What did Circle invite you to take in?

3. What was the color you engaged with during the meditation? Describe your experience.

4. What sounds and vibrations, smells and fragrant aromas did you connect with? Describe your experience as you engaged your senses within your garden.

5. After reading this chapter, were you able to create a personal space that provides support and comfort? In what ways were you able to identify and incorporate Circle within your space?

CHAPTER 5
BREAK FREE FROM LINEAR PRACTICES

Our Lives on the Line

Oh line,
You seem so efficient, so direct
Start to finish—beginning to end.
Point A to Point B.
You get straight to the point.

But what did we miss as we moved
With eyes straight ahead, focused on our goals?
What was to our left and right,
  above and below,
    as we made progress through our day?
What did we forget?

We forgot to step outside to smell the
  fresh morning air.
To look up and watch a flock of birds in flight.
To listen to the sounds of morning birdsong.

And as our day continued, we missed out on
    a deep conversation with a friend—
        one who needed support
        on this particular day.
We didn't remember our drive home or notice
The person standing by their car
On the side of the road—
    the person whose phone died,
    who needed someone to call
    for assistance on their behalf.

We collapsed into bed without stepping outside
    to gaze at the star-filled sky or the full moon.
Or listen to the night song of the crickets.
Or pause to breathe and
    listen to our own heartbeat.

The blessings and opportunities went unnoticed
In our striving for
    completion
        and accomplishment.
We forgot ourselves and ALL OTHER.

LIVING IN A LINEAR-FOCUSED SOCIETY

Living in relationship with Circle can be beneficial. Yet, most of the time as human beings, we engage more with line than with Circle in our daily lives. We start our day, immediately beginning our routines, taking on our to-do list, and moving through our day checking off boxes.

> **We come to the end of the day, collapsing into a restless sleep—only to do the same the following day, until years go by without acknowledgment, awareness, or self-reflection.**

We go through our days blindly and unconsciously. We can miss opportunities as well as potential for harm. Stuck on autopilot, we are unaware of what is truly going on around us. Approaching life in a linear fashion, we have a singular focus of achieving the goals of the day, the week, or the year.

Living in this way, we start our day with a certain level of energy and finish only when we are totally exhausted. We may become so focused on reaching our goals that we lose sight or pass by other opportunities and blessings that life offers. We allow our mind's focus to override our body's needs—oftentimes to the point that our body breaks down from illness or injury.

> **This linear path is ingrained in our society, making us believe that this is what leads to a successful, fulfilling life. Instead, we find ourselves out of balance, unfulfilled, and depleted.**

You can't help but wonder,

Did you get where you were going but missed the depth of the journey?

Circle as a Lifepath

Oh Circle,
You give us a 360-degree view of life.
You provide us with a roadmap that
    takes in our surroundings
As we move toward our goals.

We gather energy and continue around our day
Moving at a pace and with awareness to consider
    where we've been and where we're going.
Our history serves our next steps.

We can be present to the unplanned and unexpected
    without being thrown off course.
We can take in the gifts and possibilities
    that present themselves
And consider what adjustments to our day
    we may need to make.

*A song on the radio can offer us
    a message for our day.
Butterflies, dragonflies, ladybugs
    put smiles on our face.
Nature's gifts bring us a sense of peace and calm.
People who show up create moments of connection.
The food we ingest for sustenance
    is enjoyed and appreciated mindfully.*

*Time seems to expand and make room for
    moments of delight and contemplation.
We feel supported and lifted up throughout our day.
And when our head hits the pillow at night,
We feel gratitude for all we experienced,
    for our progress and our accomplishments.
We sense we are never alone,
Peacefully aware of ourselves and ALL OTHER.*

REMEMBERING HOW TO

Most of us have forgotten the ways of our ancestors. Life itself is based on circular rhythms: the moon, seasons, years, lifetimes, and generations. All build on one another, even though we refer to each as having a beginning and an end. Instead, these are cycles that start and complete another revolution within the Circle of Life.

If we apply Circle's Universal Laws and Principles to our everyday life, we choose to slow down and become fully aware that life is made up of continuous learning, growth, movement, change, transformation, and evolution. When working in a circular process, we learn from and build upon the knowledge gained through history and experience, each revolution gathering information, bringing change.

WORK WITHIN CIRCLE

When we begin our day engaged with Circle, we allow ourselves time to consider our day. We begin with the same to-do's and obligations, but rather than jump in immediately, we take a moment of gratitude and consciously choose to remain open and aware of the unexpected that may arise during our day. This awareness allows us to see from more of a 360-degree perspective—including what's happened in the past, what is happening in the present, and where we want to go in the future. We take in the possibilities available to us and remain alert to overcoming any challenges that arise. Staying engaged with Circle throughout our day, we end our day feeling tired but not overrun. And at the end of our day, we consciously pause to reflect on what happened, reviewing what worked or didn't work and what we might do differently moving forward into the days ahead. We acknowledge our day with gratitude.

Circle Holds Us

*Circle holds the finite and the infinite
Creating a lens into what is
    otherwise unimaginable
Adjusting our focus and asking us
    To slow down, observe, and enter...*

*Circle holds cooperation
    Instead of encouraging competition*

*Circle holds acceptance and compassion
    Instead of judgment and indifference*

*Circle holds self-care
    Instead of denying ourselves*

*Circle holds learning from history, experience,
    and new information
    Instead of unconsciously pushing forward*

*Circle holds being firmly grounded
    Instead of encouraging growth with no roots*

Circle holds authenticity
   Instead of promoting perfection

Circle holds mindfulness
   Instead of thoughtless action

Circle holds gratitude and appreciation
   Instead of taking ALL for granted

Circle holds the quest to seek understanding
   Instead of following the status quo

 Circle holds what serves
      and releases what is no longer necessary
   Instead of refusing to let go

Circle's Center holds the heartbeat
   of Universal Love, safety, and protection
         encouraging us
            to continue
               in our evolution.

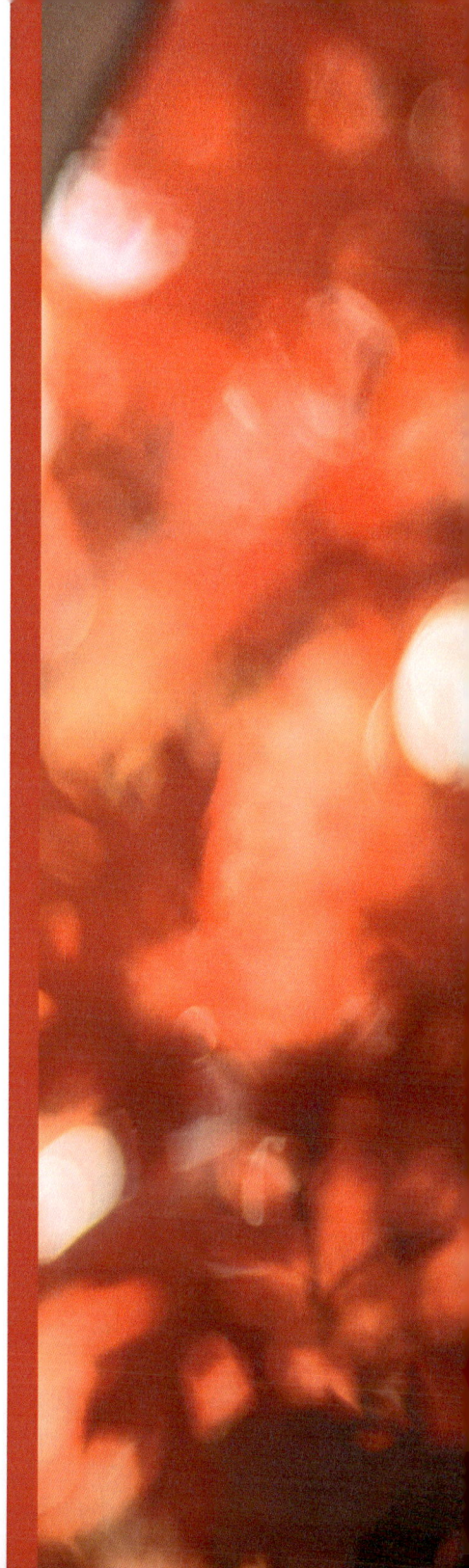

GUIDED MEDITATION

An opportunity to remember who you are within the natural process of unfolding.

Find a quiet place away from your daily responsibilities to be with the meditation's guidance. If you've created a Circle space, use that space for the meditation. To begin, take a seated position within your Circle space. Allow time for the meditation and the reflection that follows. Be sure to have your journal and pen available to record your experience.

LISTEN

Scan the QR Code for the Guided Meditation.

REFLECTION
Journaling - Connection

Life is based on circular rhythms, which repeat, yet are always evolving. The cycle of life is continually unfolding—in each moment, each day, each month, each year—just as we are. Throughout our lives, we have the opportunity to engage with this circular approach to our day-to-day living, bringing us more peace and calm, joy and gratitude.

1. When you first visualized the patterns and colors within the kaleidoscope, what did you see? What did you feel?

2. When you shifted the imagery, what new designs and colors appeared? How did they impact you?

3. As you were surrounded by the patterns and colors, what did you experience around and within yourself? Be sure to consider your senses and your emotions.

4. How did this experience transform you? In what ways did you feel different from before you began the meditation?

5. After reading this chapter, what did you learn about yourself and the ways you move through your days? In what ways might you approach your days different in the future?

CIRCLE WISDOM

BEYOND THIS BOOK

A Kaleidoscope Life

Turn, turn, turn.
Blue, green, pink, yellow, orange, purple, red.
Squares, diamonds, triangles,
Ovals, rectangles, circles.
   Ahh!

Turn, turn, turn.
Flowers, leaves, stars, rays, moonbeams of light.
Vibrant jewels dancing and moving.
Prisms of color dropping into place.
   Ahh!

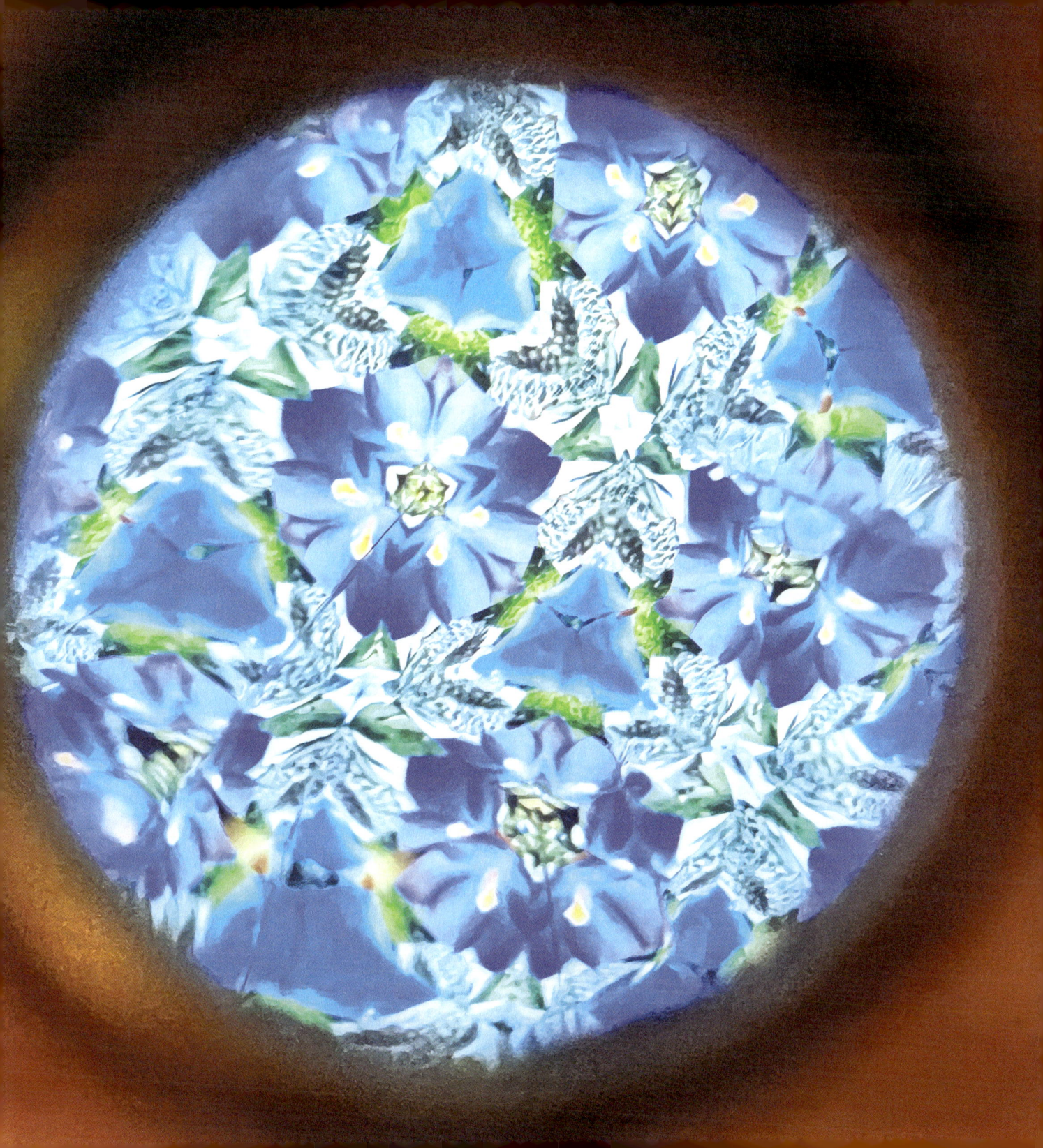

*Turn, turn, turn.
What was is no more.*

*Perplexing? Sometimes.
Better? Maybe.
Different? Definitely.
Beautiful? Always,
    Even when disbelief overshadows.*

*Every element remains. Every facet still present.
Glorious shades and shapes of refracted light.
No new parts but all transformed.
Ever-evolving, ever-rotating, ever-changing.*

*Momentarily pausing to be in the wonder
Of all that is now—
    A kaleidoscope life.*

GRATITUDE & CIRCLE'S LESSONS

Grateful for Circle's Blessings

We are grateful for the lessons that were so kindly shared by Circle and Mama Earth through the words and imagery that were given and received. In compiling what has been presented, we ourselves have come to new understandings that deepened our relationship with Circle in profound ways. What a wonderful blessing that Circle's lessons are infinite and ongoing!

Our Intention in Sharing Circle with You

It has been our intention that sharing Circle Wisdom would create a greater awareness of the vibrant, living world around you and provide opportunities to interact differently with it—being able to engage with the practical application of Circle within your daily life. Circle keeps giving, providing experiences, information, and growth. It reminds us that nature lives in a cyclical manner and we are not separate from it. These ideas are not foreign to any of us, but may have been buried under layers of historical programming and modern cultural norms.

Our intention is that Circle's lessons uncovered some of those layers that had dampened your inner knowing and began to feel familiar—like coming home.

INFINITE & ONGOING

Circle reminds us of both our uniqueness and our connection to the whole. When we live in a less linear way and stay in flow, we become more fully present to our lives. Circle provides a supportive tool that embraces us fully, helping us through pain and suffering, as well as connecting us with joy and gratitude. We begin to discover who we are within the whole, creating a fuller life experience and compelling us to be more engaged not only with ourselves and our families, but also our communities and all BEings of Mama Earth.

At its deepest roots, Circle reminds us we are ALL ONE. Returning to Circle Wisdom benefits all BEings and allows us to move forward in our evolutionary process. To enhance our humanity. To become more. To elevate our relationship with the Divine.

Gratitude to the Reader

Once again, we thank you for joining us to experience Circle and its beingness. We encourage you to return to the words, imagery, and meditations as often as possible, taking its wisdom deeper into your life and sharing it with others.

May you feel through your entire being Circle's blessing, enwrapping YOU always in a blanket of Unconditional Love.

GRATITUDE TO OUR MENTOR, TEACHER, AND FRIEND:
Janet Diederichs

Our hearts are overflowing with gratitude for Janet's many years of guidance and mentorship. Without the teachings and time spent in group Circle, private mentoring, and support from our teacher and guide, this book would not have been possible. We are blessed beyond measure to have the privilege to share the lessons that she has so patiently and lovingly taught us.

When this journey began with Janet, we were unaware of the overwhelming impact Circle's Wisdom would have upon our lives. Through the years, we have experienced firsthand what it means to be embraced by Circle. Even when we didn't understand how we were being held by Circle, Janet's guidance, presence, and availability showed us Circle's BEingness. She carefully planted Seeds of Light within our hearts and minds, always prompting us to feel the lessons within every cell of our bodies.

As those seeds have taken hold and grown, we've experienced what it means to be broken open—to shine light on our deepest shadows and expose our truest selves. Through Janet's teachings and Circle's Wisdom, we've learned that tending to our internal garden is an ongoing process. One that requires nurturance of what we want to grow and release of what no longer serves us. Although this path is not always easy or clear, it is one we are committed to follow for the rest of our lives.

We are both forever grateful for Janet's life, wisdom, teachings, and BEingness. Thank you and bless you.

Donna Mazzitelli and Melissa McQueen

Students of Janet Diederichs, Circle Wisdom and Universal Beingness Within The Whole

ADDITIONAL RESOURCES:

Janet Diederichs

With a deep love of plants, pets, and nature, Janet Diederichs is committed to environmental guardianship and focused on the many modalities within the healing arts. As an ongoing student, she is open to serve as mentor and spiritual counselor within the philosophy of *Universal Beingness Within the Whole.*

janetdiederichs.com

Donna Mazzitelli

Through *Writing with Donna,* Donna Mazzitelli provides intimate, sacred writing retreats, coaching, and editing services. Her work is infused with a strong bond with nature and intuitive guidance to help writers discover their sacred message and write from their heart center. *Merry Dissonance Press*, a hybrid publisher founded by Donna, offers a boutique experience focused on collaboration to bring into the world works of Light.

writingwithdonna.com | merrydissonancepress.com

Melissa McQueen

Creative Reflections Design, owned by Melissa McQueen, brings her beautiful soul and light-filled essence to her work. Through visual artistry, website development, and graphic design, she focuses on reflecting her client's energy and personality. She also partners with her husband and accomplished musician, Danny, in the creative works shared through *SoulSoundImages,* a marketplace of nature photography, art, and music with the vision of connecting to your senses through the heart.

creativereflections.design | soulsoundimages.com

Seeds of Light for ALL

SeedsOfLightForALL.com is a website created to extend beyond the teachings of this book, allowing visitors the opportunity to further expand their knowledge, increase their awareness, and receive continued experiences with Circle and the philosophy of Universal Beingness Within the Whole.

seedsoflightforall.com

DIVE DEEPER: SUGGESTED READINGS

Braiding Sweetgrass: Indigenous Wisdom, Scientific Knowledge and the Teachings of Plants, by Robin Wall Kimmerer. Milkweed Editions, 2015.

Business Revolution through Ancestral Wisdom, by Tú Moonwalker, JoAnne O'Brien-Levin, Ph.D, and Láné Sáan Moonwalker. Outskirts Press, 2008.

Noticing, by Kobi Yumada and Elise Hurst. Compendium, 2023

The Light Eaters: How the Unseen World of Plant Intelligence Offers a New Understanding of Life on Earth, by Zoë Schlanger. HarperCollins Publishers, 2024.

Additional book recommendations listed on our website: seedsoflightforall.com

MORE BOOKS TO COME!

TREE WISDOM

RAINBOW WISDOM

THANK YOU

FOR BEE-ing!